Safety at Home

Acknowledgments
Executive Editor: Diane Sharpe
Supervising Editor: Stephanie Muller
Design Manager: Sharon Golden
Page Design: Ian Winton
Photography: Norman McBeath: 9, 13; Alex Ramsay: cover (both),
17, 21, 23, 29.

ISBN 0-8114-3723-X

Copyright © 1995 Steck-Vaughn Company.

1 2 3 4 5 6 7 8 9 00 PO 00 99 98 97 96 95 94

Safety
at
Home

Helena Ramsay

Illustrated by

Derek Brazell

STECK-VAUGHN
COMPANY
ELEMENTARY • SECONDARY • ADULT • LIBRARY

We have to make sure our house is safe for her.

There are things in every house that could hurt babies and children. Safety at home is very important.

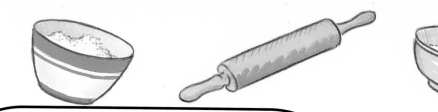

I'll put the cupcakes in the oven. We can't let Amy touch the oven door. It's very hot.

Never touch an oven when it is on. You could get burned.

Never stand too close
to a stove. You could
be splashed with boiling
water or very hot oil.

Even adults have to be careful with knives and scissors. It's very easy to cut yourself.

Never touch an iron.
It gets very hot.

Electric sockets are very dangerous.
Never touch them or try to put
anything in them.

15

Plastic bags can be dangerous.
If a child put one over her head,
she would not be able to breathe.

17

Never play with matches.
You could burn yourself or
start a fire.

Never get too close to a fire.
You could get burned.

22

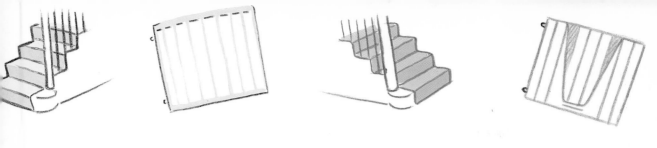

Never leave things on the stairs.
Someone could trip over them
and get hurt.

23

24

Yes, let's put these cleaning liquids up high so Amy can't reach them.

Medicines can be dangerous, too. Never touch them unless an adult gives them to you.

25

26

Always walk down stairs
carefully so you don't fall.

27

Please watch Amy!

Home is a safe place for everyone, as long as we are careful.

Here is a room in someone's home. What would you do to make it safe for a young child?

Index